What's My Style?

I love creating elaborate patterns packed with detail so I can do lots of intricate coloring. I try to use as many colors as possible. Then I layer on lots of fun details. Here are some more examples of my work.

My studio is filled with natural light, tons of coloring supplies, and lots of inspiration, all of which motivate me to create and color!

Where to Start

You might find putting color on a fresh page stressful. It's okay! Here are a few tricks I use to get the ink flowing.

Start with an easy decision. If a design has leaves, without a doubt, that's where I start. No matter how wacky and colorful everything else gets, I always color the leaves in my illustrations green. I have no reason for it; it's just how it is! Try to find something in the design to help ground you by making an easy color decision: leaves are green, the sky is blue, etc.

Get inspired. Take a good look at everything in the illustration. You chose to color it for a reason. One little piece that you love will jump out and say, "Color me! Use red, please!" Or maybe it will say blue, or pink, or green. Just relax—it will let you know.

Follow your instincts. What colors do you love? Are you a big fan of purple? Or maybe yellow is your favorite. If you love it, use it!

Just go for it. Close your eyes, pick up a color, point to a spot on the illustration, and start! Sometimes starting is the hardest part, but it's the fastest way to finish!

Helpful Hints

There is no right or wrong. All colors work together, so don't be scared to mix it up. The results can be surprising!

Try it. Test your chosen colors on scrap paper before you start coloring your design. You can also test blending techniques and how to use different shapes and patterns for detail work—you can see how different media will blend with or show up on top of your chosen colors. I even use the paper to clean my markers or pens if necessary.

Make a color chart. A color chart is like a test paper for every single color you have! It provides a more accurate way to choose colors than selecting them based on the color of the marker's cap. To make a color chart, color a swatch with each marker, colored pencil, gel pen, etc. Label each swatch with the name or number of the marker so you can easily find it later.

Do you like warm colors?

How about cool colors?

Maybe you like warm and cool colors together!

Keep going. Even if you think you've ruined a piece, work through it. I go through the same cycle with my coloring: I love a piece at the beginning, and by the halfway point I nearly always dislike it. Sometimes by the end I love it again, and sometimes I don't, and that's okay. It's important to remember that you're coloring for you— no one else. If you really don't like a piece at the end, stash it away and remember that you learned something. You know what not to do next time. My studio drawers are full of everything from duds to masterpieces!

Be patient. Let markers, gel pens, and paints dry thoroughly between each layer. There's nothing worse than smudging a cluster of freshly inked dots across the page with your hand. Just give them a minute to dry and then you can move on to the next layer.

Use caution. Juicy/inky markers can "spit" when you uncap them. Open them away from your art piece.

Work from light to dark. It's much easier to make something darker gradually than to lighten it.

Shade with gray. A mid-tone lavender-gray marker is perfect for adding shadows to your artwork, giving it depth and making it pop right off the page!

Try blending fluid. If you like working with alcohol-based markers, a refillable bottle of blending fluid or a blending pen is a great investment. Aside from enabling you to easily blend colors together, it can help clean up unwanted splatters or mistakes—it may not take some colors away completely, but it will certainly lighten them. I use it to clean the body of my markers as I'm constantly smudging them with inky fingers. When a marker is running out of ink, I find adding a few drops of blending fluid to the ink barrel will make it last a bit longer.

Layering and Blending

I love layering and blending colors. It's a great way to create shading and give your finished piece lots of depth and dimension. The trick is to work from the lightest color to the darkest and then go over everything again with the lightest shade to keep the color smooth and bring all the layers together.

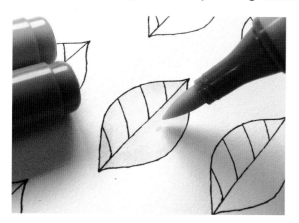

1 Apply a base layer with the lightest color.

2 Add the middle color, using it to create shading.

3 Smooth out the color by going over everything with the lightest color.

4 Add the darkest color, giving your shading even more depth. Use the middle color to go over the same area you colored in Step 2.

5 Go over everything with the lightest color as you did in Step 3.

Patterning and Details

Layering and blending will give your coloring depth and dimension. Adding patterning and details will really bring it to life. If you're not convinced, try adding a few details to one of your colored pieces with a white gel pen—that baby will make magic happen! Have fun adding all of the dots, doodles, and swirls you can imagine.

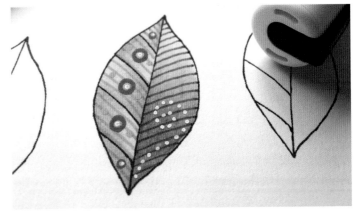

1 Once you've finished your coloring, blending, and layering, go back and add simple patterning like lines or dots. You can add your patterns in black or color. For this leaf, I used two different shades of green pen.

2 Now it's time to add some fun details using paint pens or gel pens. Here I used white, yellow, and more green.

This design really pops with lots of patterning and little details.

Coloring Supplies

I'm always asked about the mediums I use to color my illustrations. The answer would be really long if I listed every single thing, so here are a few of my favorites. Keep in mind that these are *my* favorites. When you color, you should use YOUR favorites!

Alcohol-based markers. I have many, and a variety of brands. My favorites have a brush nib—it's so versatile. A brush nib is perfect for tiny, tight corners, but is also able to cover a large, open space easily. I find I rarely get streaking, and if I do, it's usually because the ink is running low!

Fine-tip pens. Just like with markers, I have lots of different pens. I use them for my layers of detail work and for the itsy bitsy spots my markers can't get into.

Paint pens. These are wonderful! Because the ink is usually opaque, they stand out really well against a dark base color. I use extra fine point pens for their precision. Some paint pens are water based, so I can use a brush to blend the colors and create a cool watercolor effect.

Gel pens. I have a few, but I usually stick to white and neon colors that will stand out on top of dark base colors or other mediums.

Hello Angel #1275 Sweet Sloth: markers, pens, paint pens, colored pencils

Hello Angel #1266 Seaspray Vacay: markers, pens, paint pen:

Hello Angel #1267 A Little Bubbly: markers, pens, paint pens, colored pencils

  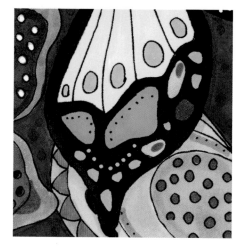

Hello Angel #1268 Never Too Many: markers, pens, paint pens

Hello Angel #1269 Eye on You: markers, pens, paint pens

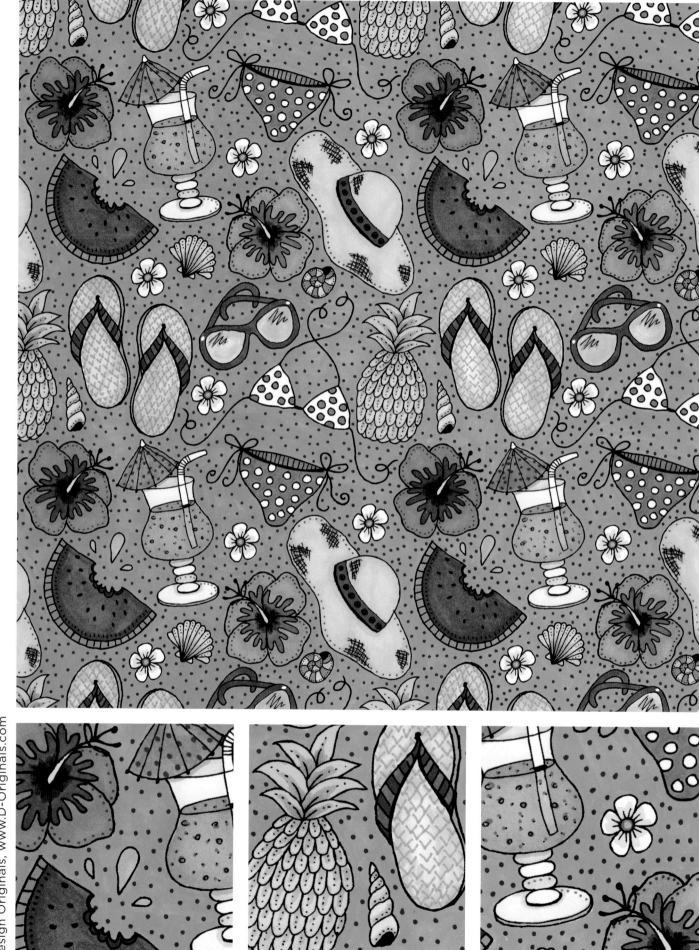

Hello Angel #1270 I Spy...Summer: markers, pens, paint pens

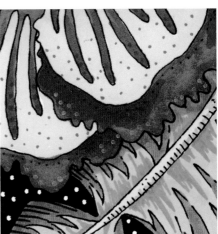

Hello Angel #1271 Tropical Tableau: markers, pens, paint pens

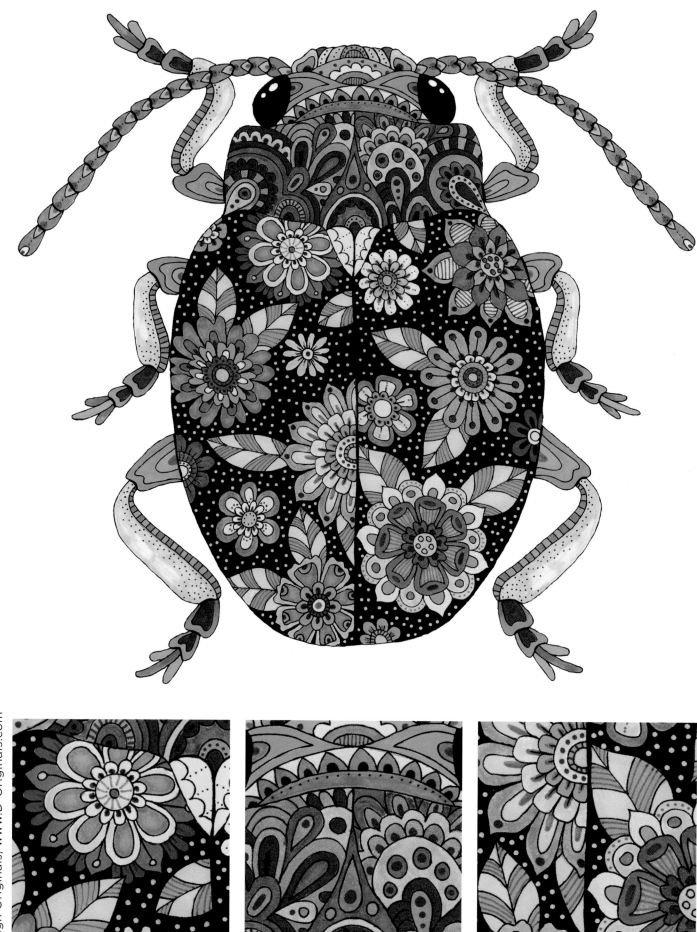

Hello Angel #1272 Cute As a Bug: markers, pens, paint pens

And 'tis my faith that every flower
Enjoys the air it breathes.

—WILLIAM WORDSWORTH,
"LINES WRITTEN IN EARLY SPRING"

Nature always wears
the colors of the spirit.

—Ralph Waldo Emerson

When life hands you pineapples, make a piña colada.

—Unknown

She ran away in her sleep
And dreamed of paradise
Every time she closed her eyes.

—COLDPLAY, "PARADISE"

A pineapple a day
keeps the worry away.

—UNKNOWN

Travel and change of place
impart new vigor to the mind.

—SENECA

The best way to observe a fish is to become a fish.

—JACQUES COUSTEAU

_____
_____
_____
_____
_____
_____
_____
_____

There's a place you want to go.
It's a beach so Wayo that
only locals know. Take a break,
you're in paradise, so relax
under tropical night skies.

—FIGHT FAIR, "WAYO BEACH"

You can't get much more hot pink than these flowers!
Notice how the wavy pink shapes
balance out the sharp green fern leaves.

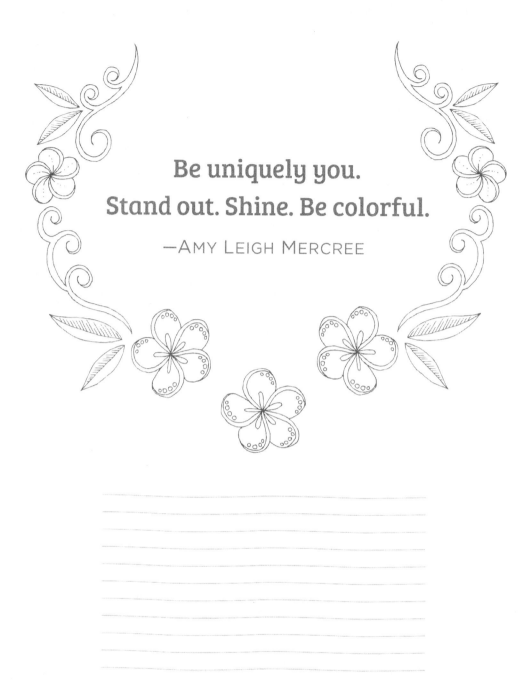

Be uniquely you.
Stand out. Shine. Be colorful.

—AMY LEIGH MERCREE

Hello Angel #1265 Toucantemplation

Mark the transition between shore and sea boldly,
as with these white bubbles frothing off a deep blue surf.

Some of the best memories
are made in flip flops.

—KELLIE ELMORE

Having a plan helps: see how an analogous scheme
of blues and greens delineates scales?

The Rainbow Fish
shared his scales left and right.
And the more he gave away, the more delighted he became.

—MARCUS PFISTER, *THE RAINBOW FISH*

_____
_____
_____
_____
_____
_____
_____
_____
_____

Hello Angel #1267 A Little Bubbly

Show who's flying above who by alternating warm and cool color schemes.

Butterflies are
self-propelled flowers.

—Robert A. Heinlein

Stack shades and tints of the same color
to make this flamingo utterly beautiful.

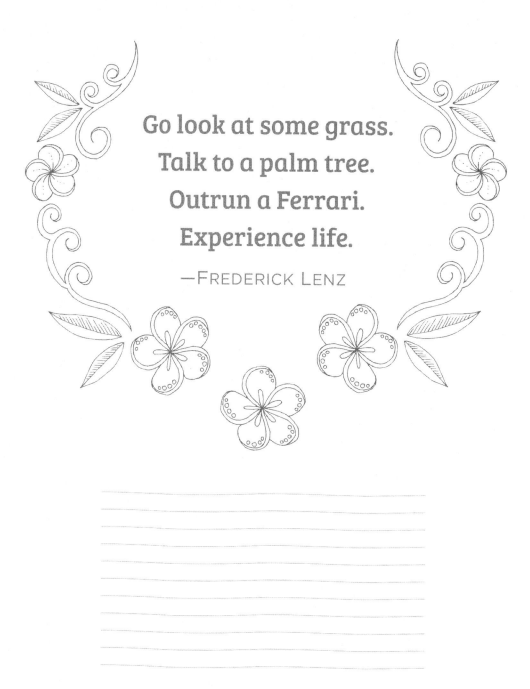

Go look at some grass.
Talk to a palm tree.
Outrun a Ferrari.
Experience life.

—FREDERICK LENZ

Hello Angel #1269 Eye on You

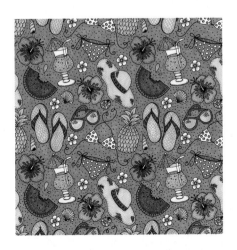

Try flattening your background with one color
and then roughing it up with dots. The objects
seem to float off the page by contrast.

Let the waves kiss your feet
and the sand be your seat.

—UNKNOWN

Hello Angel #1270 I Spy...Summer

Some well-placed greens and yellows buttress the blooming complementary colors in the foreground of this piece.

Paradise is always where love dwells.

—JEAN PAUL

Hello Angel #1271 Tropical Tableau

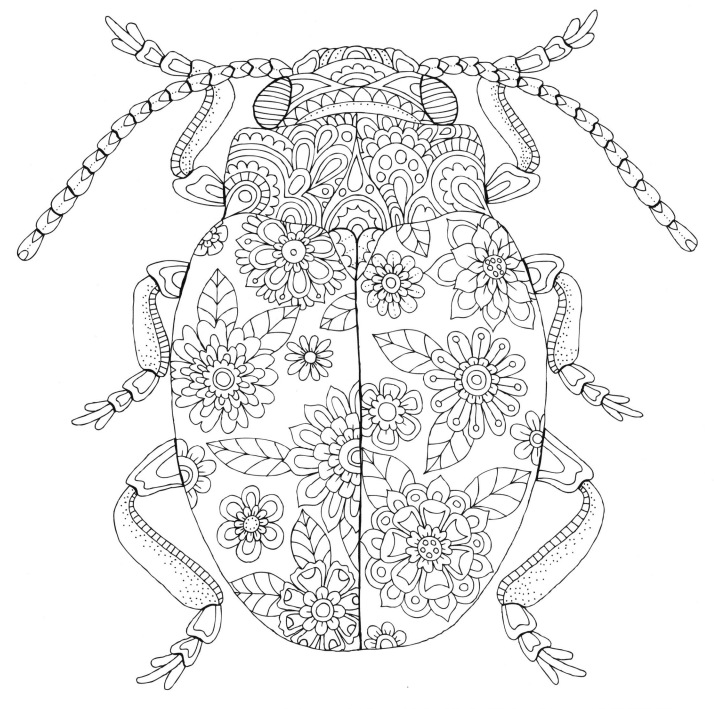

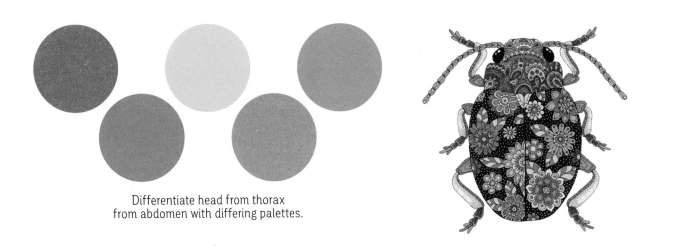

Differentiate head from thorax
from abdomen with differing palettes.

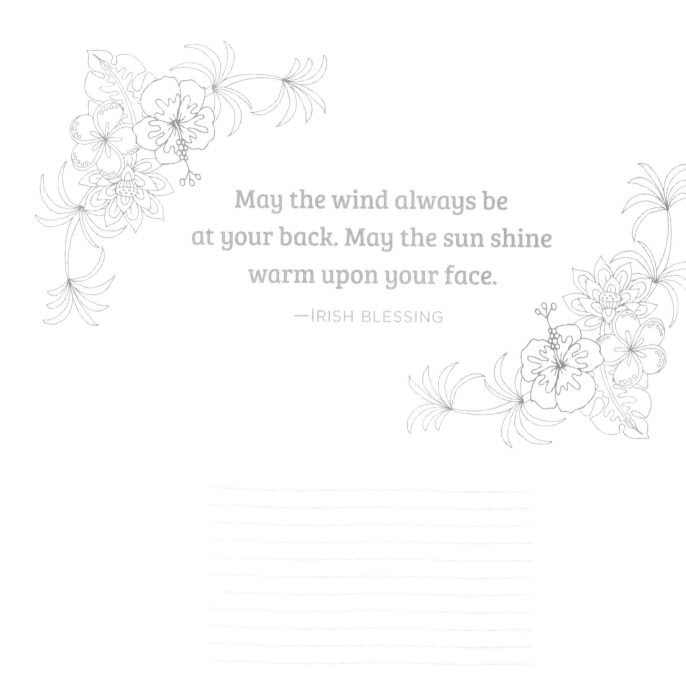

May the wind always be
at your back. May the sun shine
warm upon your face.

—IRISH BLESSING

Hello Angel #1272 Cute As a Bug

And the turtles, of course...
all the turtles are free, as turtles and,
maybe, all creatures should be.

—Dr. Seuss, *Yertle the Turtle and Other Stories*

The sea is as near as we come
to another world.

—ANNE STEVENSON

You must live in the present,
launch yourself on every wave,
find your eternity in each moment.

—HENRY DAVID THOREAU

The happiness of the bee and
the dolphin is to exist. For man it is
to know that and to wonder at it.

—JACQUES COUSTEAU

Try to be like the turtle—
at ease in your own shell.

—BILL COPELAND

One cannot collect all the
beautiful shells on the beach;
one can collect only a few,
and they are more beautiful
if they are few.

—ANNE MORROW LINDBERGH,
GIFT FROM THE SEA

Take a look above you.
Discover the view. If you haven't noticed, please do.

—JIM HENSON,
"I WONDER 'BOUT THE WORLD ABOVE UP THERE"

Just look at the world around you
Right here on the ocean floor
Such wonderful things surround you
What more is you lookin' for?

—"UNDER THE SEA,"
THE LITTLE MERMAID

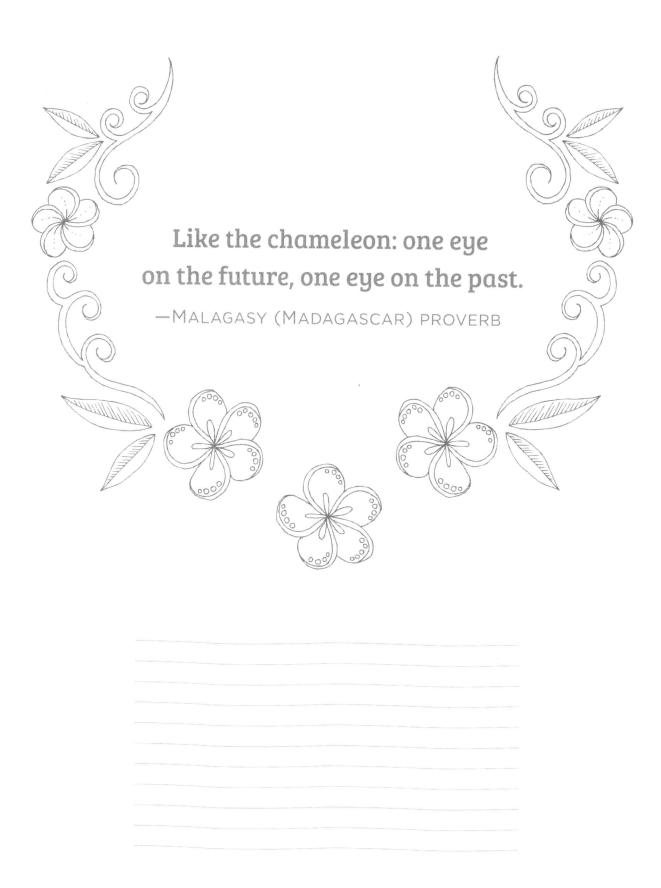

Like the chameleon: one eye
on the future, one eye on the past.

—MALAGASY (MADAGASCAR) PROVERB

Palm trees, ocean breeze,
salty air, sun-kissed hair...
that endless summer, take me there.

—Unknown

The sea, once it casts its spell,
holds one in its net of wonder forever.

—JACQUES COUSTEAU

At the beach, life is different.
Time doesn't move hour to hour
but mood to moment. We live by
the currents, plan by the tides,
and follow the sun.

—SANDY GINGRAS

Some beach, somewhere.
There's a big umbrella casting shade
over an empty chair. Palm trees are
growing and a warm breeze a-blowing.
I picture myself right there,
on some beach, somewhere.

—BLAKE SHELTON,
"SOME BEACH"

The dance of the palm trees,
the oceans calling, the first rays of sun,
and heaven is here.

—MICHAEL DOLAN

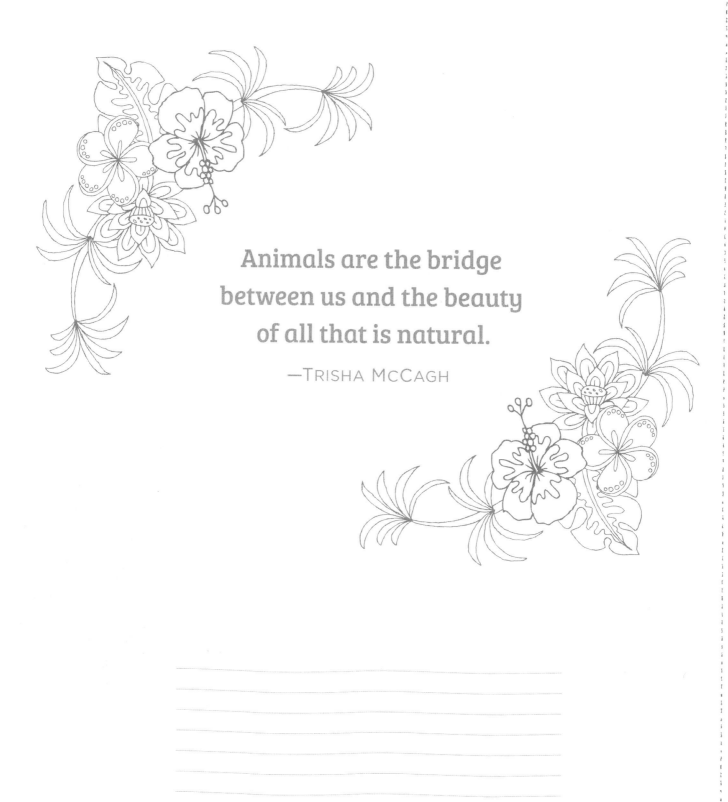

Animals are the bridge
between us and the beauty
of all that is natural.

—Trisha McCagh

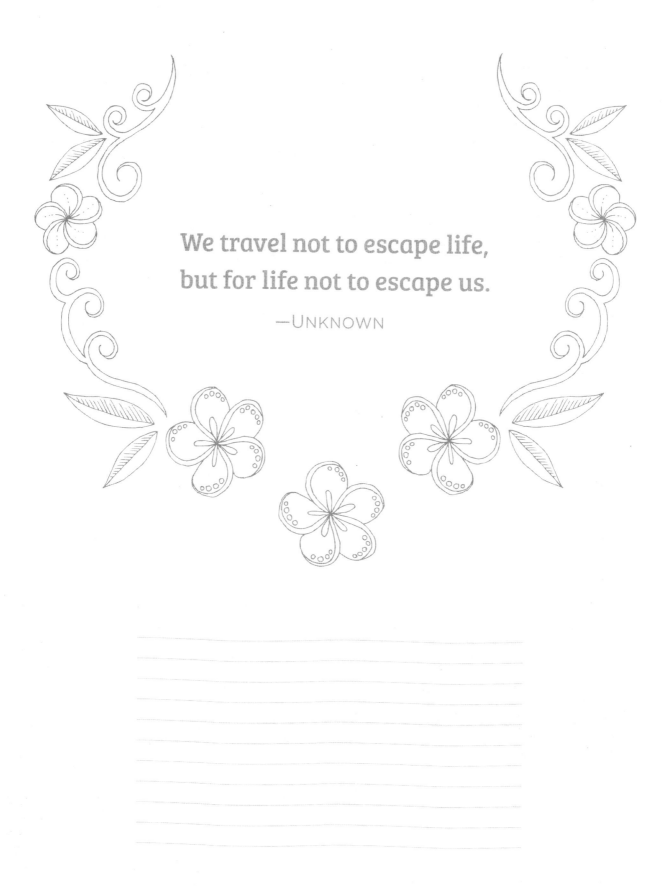

We travel not to escape life,
but for life not to escape us.

—UNKNOWN